Quick
CAKES

KÖNEMANN

Quick Mix Cakes

Remember those Saturday afternoons at Grandma's when the smell of freshly baked cakes filled the kitchen? Most of us believe that making a cake requires too much time and skill. Think again. If you have a mixing bowl, wooden spoon and a few stock ingredients, then this is the book for you.

Sour Cream Chocolate Cake

Preparation time:
  15 minutes
Total cooking time:
  35–40 minutes
Makes one ring cake

1 cup sugar
1³/4 cups self-rising flour
2/3 cup cocoa powder
1 teaspoon baking soda
1/4 cup vegetable oil
3/4 cup sour cream
2/3 cup water
2 eggs

1. Preheat the oven to moderate 350°F. Brush a deep, 8 inch bundt or ring pan with melted butter or oil.
2. Place all the ingredients in a food processor. Process in short bursts until the mixture is well combined and has a smooth texture.
3. Spoon the mixture evenly into the prepared pan. Bake for 35–40 minutes, or until a skewer comes out clean when inserted into the center of the cake. Leave the cake in the pan for 10 minutes before turning onto a wire rack to cool. Drizzle with Rich Chocolate Icing (see page 63), if you like.

Note: Sour Cream Chocolate Cake is delicious served as a dessert with freshly whipped cream or ice cream and fresh berries.

Sour Cream Chocolate Cake

Sticky Date and Gingerbread Cake

Preparation time:
  25 minutes
Total cooking time:
  50–60 minutes
Makes one oblong cake

4 oz butter
*3/4 cup golden syrup
  or dark corn syrup*
1 cup sugar
2 cups all-purpose
  flour, sifted
1 teaspoon baking
  soda
3 teaspoons ground
  ginger
1 teaspoon pumpkin
  pie spice
*1/4 teaspoon ground
  cloves*
2 eggs
1 cup milk
*1 1/2 cups chopped
  pitted dates*

1. Preheat the oven to warm 315°F. Lightly grease an 8 x 12 inch pan and line the base and sides with waxed paper.
2. Combine the butter and syrup in a large pan and stir over low heat without boiling until the butter has melted. Add the sugar, flour, soda, spices, eggs and milk. Whisk until the mixture is smooth.
3. Sprinkle the dates over the base of the pan and pour the cake mixture over the top. Bake for 50–60 minutes, or until a skewer comes out clean when inserted in the center of the cake. Set aside for 5 minutes before turning onto a wire rack to cool. Lightly dust with confectioners' sugar and serve the cake warm or cold.

Lemon Coconut Cake

Preparation time:
  20 minutes
Total cooking time:
  40 minutes
Makes one round cake

*1 1/2 cups self-rising
  flour*
*1/2 cup shredded
  coconut*
1 tablespoon grated
  lemon rind
1 cup sugar
4 oz butter, melted
2 eggs
1 cup milk

Coconut Icing
*1 1/2 cups confectioners'
  sugar, sifted*
1 cup shredded
  coconut
*1/2 teaspoon grated
  lemon rind*
1/4 cup lemon juice

1. Preheat the oven to moderate 350°F. Brush a deep, 8 inch round cake pan with melted butter or oil. Line the base and side with waxed paper.
2. Combine the flour, coconut, rind, sugar, butter, eggs and milk in a large bowl and mix well with a wooden spoon until smooth.
3. Pour the mixture into the pan and bake for 40 minutes, or until a skewer comes out clean when inserted in the center of the cake. Set the cake aside for 3 minutes before turning onto a wire rack to cool. When the cake is cold, spread with Coconut Icing.
4. **To make Coconut Icing:** Combine the confectioners' sugar and coconut in a bowl. Add the rind and enough juice to make a stiff but spreadable icing. Lemon Coconut Cake is pictured garnished with some candied lemon slices.

*Lemon Coconut Cake (top) with
Sticky Date and Gingerbread Cake*

Spicy Pumpkin and Cardamom Ring

Preparation time:
  20 minutes
Total cooking time:
  40 minutes
Makes one ring cake

4 oz butter,
  softened
1/2 cup light brown
  sugar
2 eggs
1 1/4 cups self-rising
  flour
1 1/2 teaspoons ground
  cardamom
3/4 cup cold cooked
  mashed pumpkin
2 tablespoons golden
  syrup or dark corn
  syrup
1/2 cup pitted
  chopped dates

1. Preheat the oven to moderate 350°F. Grease a deep, 8 inch bundt or ring pan with oil or butter.
2. Combine all the ingredients in a large mixing bowl and beat with electric beaters on low speed until well combined. Increase the speed of the beaters to medium and beat for about 2 minutes more or until the mixture is smooth and has changed color.
3. Spoon the mixture into the pan and smooth the top with a spatula. Bake for 40 minutes, or until a skewer comes out clean when inserted in the center of the cake. Set aside for 5 minutes, then turn onto a wire rack to cool. Serve sprinkled with confectioners' sugar, or spread with a Glacé Icing (see page 61) of your choice.

Apricot and Coconut Rolls

Preparation time:
  30 minutes
Total cooking time:
  50 minutes
Makes two rolls

2/3 cup chopped
  dried apricots
4 oz butter, softened
3/4 cup confectioners'
  sugar
2 eggs
1 cup self-rising
  flour
1/2 cup all-purpose
  flour
1/4 cup shredded
  coconut
1/3 cup milk

1. Cover the apricots with boiling water; set aside for 20 minutes, then drain well. Preheat the oven to moderate 350°F. Grease two 3 x 8 inch bread molds.
2. Combine the remaining ingredients in a large bowl and beat with electric beaters on low speed until all the ingredients are combined. Increase the speed to medium and beat for about 2 minutes more, or until the mixture is smooth and has changed color. Stir the apricots through the mixture.
3. Divide the mixture evenly between the prepared molds, cover with the greased lids and place on a baking sheet. Bake upright for 50 minutes, or until a skewer comes out clean when inserted in the center of the rolls. Set aside for 10 minutes before turning onto a wire rack to cool. Serve the rolls either warm or cold, sliced.

Variation: Use glacé apricots or peaches instead of dried apricots, if preferred.

Spicy Pumpkin and Cardamom Ring (top) with Apricot and Coconut Rolls

Sour Cream Cupcakes

Preparation time:
  25 minutes
Total cooking time:
  15–20 minutes
Makes 22

4³/4 oz butter
¹/2 cup sugar
1 teaspoon vanilla
  extract
2 eggs, lightly
  beaten
²/3 cup sour
  cream
1¹/4 cups
  self-rising flour
¹/4 cup rice flour

1. Preheat the oven to moderate 350°F. Place paper liners in two 12-cup muffin pans.
2. Beat the butter and sugar in a large bowl until light and creamy. Gradually beat in the vanilla extract and eggs.
3. Use a large metal spoon to fold in the sour cream and combined sifted flours, until just smooth.
4. Spoon the mixture evenly into the paper liners. Bake for 15–20 minutes, or until the cupcakes are golden on top. Test a few with a skewer—if it comes out clean they are cooked. Transfer to a wire rack to cool. Spread with Citrus Glacé (see page 61) and decorate with crystallized flowers, if you like.

Banana Nut Loaf

Preparation time:
  20 minutes
Total cooking time:
  1 hour
Makes one oblong cake

4 oz butter,
  softened
1 cup light brown
  sugar, plus
  1 tablespoon, extra
3 eggs
1¹/2 cups whole
  wheat self-rising
  flour
¹/2 cup shredded
  coconut, plus
  2 teaspoons, extra
²/3 cup mashed
  banana
¹/2 cup milk
¹/4 cup roasted
  unsalted macadamia
  nuts, chopped
¹/2 teaspoon pumpkin
  pie spice

1. Preheat the oven to moderate 350°F. Grease a 5¹/2 x 8¹/2 x 2³/4 inch loaf pan and line the base with waxed paper.
2. Combine the butter, 1 cup sugar, eggs, flour, ¹/2 cup coconut, banana and milk in a bowl and beat with electric beaters on low speed until well combined. Increase the speed to medium and beat for about 2 minutes more, or until the mixture is smooth and has changed color.
3. Spoon half the mixture into the pan. Sprinkle with half the combined nuts, spice, and remaining sugar and coconut. Top with the remaining cake mixture, smooth the surface and sprinkle with the remaining nut mixture. Bake for 1 hour, or until a skewer comes out clean when inserted in the center. You may need to cover the cake loosely with foil during cooking if the top starts to brown too much.

Note: Use 2 very ripe bananas for this recipe. The ripeness of the bananas will give the cake a sweeter flavor and lighter texture.

Sour Cream Cupcakes (top) with Banana Nut Loaf

Fruit and Bran Loaf

Preparation time:
  15 minutes +
  15 minutes soaking
Total cooking time:
  50 minutes
Makes one loaf

1¹/2 *cups mixed*
  dried chopped
  fruit (see note)
¹/2 *cup raisins*
1 *cup All Bran*
¹/2 *cup light brown*
  sugar
1¹/2 *cups milk*
1¹/2 *cups self-rising*
  flour
whole blanched
  almonds, to
  decorate

1. Lightly grease a 9 x 5¹/4 x 2³/4 inch loaf pan with melted butter or oil. Line the base with waxed paper. Place the mixed fruit, raisins, All Bran, sugar and milk in a large mixing bowl and stir to combine. Leave to soak for at least 15 minutes.
2. Preheat the oven to moderate 350°F. Add the sifted flour to the mixture and combine well. Spoon the mixture into the prepared pan and smooth the surface.

Decorate with the almonds. Bake for 45–50 minutes, or until a skewer comes out clean when inserted in the center. Set aside for 5 minutes, then turn onto a wire rack to cool. Serve plain, sliced with butter or toasted.

Note: You may use any combination of chopped dried fruits amounting to 1¹/2 cups.

Lemon Polenta Cake

Preparation time:
  30 minutes
Total cooking time:
  40 minutes
Makes one round cake

8 *oz butter*
1 *cup sugar*
¹/4 *cup grated lemon*
  rind
1 *teaspoon vanilla*
  extract
3 *eggs*
2 *tablespoons freshly*
  squeezed lemon
  juice
1¹/4 *cups ground*
  almonds
1 *cup polenta*
¹/4 *cup self-rising*
  flour

1. Preheat the oven to moderate 350°F. Brush a deep 8³/4 inch round cake pan with melted butter or oil. Line the base and sides with waxed paper. Beat the butter and sugar in a large bowl with electric beaters until light and creamy. Add the rind and vanilla extract; beat until thoroughly combined.
2. Add the eggs one at a time, beating well after each addition. The mixture will look quite curdled at this stage. Add the juice, almonds, polenta, flour and a pinch of salt. Stir until the mixture is smooth. Spoon the mixture into the prepared pan and smooth the surface. Bake for 40 minutes, or until a skewer comes out clean when inserted in the center.
3. Set the cake aside for at least 10 minutes before turning out of the pan. Drizzle with Citrus Syrup (page 58) or cut into wedges and serve warm with ice cream or thick cream.

Note: Keeps for up to 3 days in an airtight container. Reheat the cake in the microwave.

Fruit and Bran Loaf (top) with Lemon Polenta Cake

Banana Gingerbread Cake

Preparation time:
  20 minutes
Total cooking time:
  1 hour
Makes one square cake

6 oz butter
$^1/3$ cup golden syrup
  or dark corn syrup
1 cup light brown
  sugar
2 eggs
1$^1/3$ cups mashed
  banana
2$^1/2$ cups self-rising
  flour
$^1/2$ cup all-purpose
  flour
1 teaspoon baking
  soda
1 tablespoon ground
  ginger
2 teaspoons pumpkin
  pie spice
$^1/4$ teaspoon ground
  cloves
2 tablespoons
  milk

1. Preheat the oven
to moderate 350°F.
Grease a deep, 9 inch
square cake pan. Line
the base and sides with
waxed paper.
2. Beat the butter,
syrup and sugar in
a bowl until creamy.
Add the eggs; beat well
after each addition.
Beat in the banana. Sift
the flours, soda and
spices together. Beat in
alternately with milk.
3. Spoon the mixture
into the prepared pan
and smooth the surface.
Bake for 55 minutes, or
until a skewer comes
out clean when inserted
in the center of the
cake. Set aside for
3 minutes, then turn
onto a wire rack to
cool. Spread with
Lemon Ginger Glacé
(page 61) and top with
preserved or glacé
ginger, chopped.

Cinnamon Apple Cake

Preparation time:
  25 minutes
Total cooking time:
  45 minutes
Makes one round cake

6 oz butter,
  softened
$^2/3$ cup sugar
3 eggs
1 cup self-rising
  flour
$^1/2$ cup all-purpose
  flour
1 teaspoon ground
  cinnamon
$^1/3$ cup milk
1 apple, peeled, cored
  and chopped
2 teaspoons sugar
2 tablespoons orange
  marmalade

1. Preheat the oven
to moderate 350°F.
Brush a deep, 8 inch
round cake pan with
melted butter or oil.
Line the base and side
with waxed paper.
2. Combine the
butter, sugar, eggs,
flours, cinnamon and
milk in a bowl. Beat
with electric beaters
on low speed for
1 minute. Gradually
increase the speed to
medium and beat for
3 minutes more, or
until the mixture is
smooth and has
changed color.
3. Spoon the mixture
into the pan and
smooth the surface.
Scatter the apple over
the top and sprinkle
with sugar. Bake for
45 minutes, or until
a skewer comes out
clean when inserted
in the center of the
cake. Set the cake aside
for 3 minutes before
turning onto a wire
rack to cool.
4. Heat the marmalade
in a small pan or in a
microwave oven until
just melted. Brush over
the hot cake and allow
to cool before serving.

*Banana Gingerbread Cake (top) with
Cinnamon Apple Cake*

Orange Poppy Seed Cake

Preparation time:
  30 minutes
Total cooking time:
  1 hour
Makes one round cake

1¹/2 cups self-rising
  flour
1/3 cup ground
  almonds
3 tablespoons
  poppy seeds
6 oz butter
2/3 cup sugar
1/4 cup orange or
  apricot jam
2–3 teaspoons finely
  grated orange rind
1/3 cup orange juice
3 eggs

Icing
3¹/3 oz butter
3¹/3 oz cream cheese
1 cup confectioners'
  sugar, sifted
1–2 teaspoons freshly
  squeezed lemon
  juice or vanilla
  extract

1. Preheat the oven
to moderate 350°F.
Brush a deep, 8 inch
round cake pan with
melted butter or oil.
Line the base and side
with waxed paper.
Sift the flour into a
large bowl and add
the almonds and

poppy seeds. Make a
well in the center.
2. Place the butter,
sugar, jam, rind and
juice in a pan. Stir
over low heat until the
butter has melted and
the mixture is smooth.
Gradually add the
butter mixture to the
dry ingredients, stirring
with a whisk until
smooth. Add the
eggs and whisk until
well combined.
3. Pour the mixture
into the prepared
pan and bake for
50–60 minutes, or
until a skewer comes
out clean when inserted
in the center of the
cake. Set aside for at
least 15 minutes before
turning onto a wire
rack to cool.
4. To make Icing:
Beat the butter and
cream cheese with
electric beaters until
smooth. Add the
confectioners' sugar
and juice or extract
gradually and beat
until thick and creamy.
Spread the Icing over
the cooled cake.
Decorate with strips
of orange rind if
you wish.

Note: This cake is
also delicious drizzled
with Citrus Syrup
(see page 58). Pour
the cooled syrup over
the warm cake.

Honey Pecan Spice Loaf

Preparation time:
  20 minutes
Total cooking time:
  55 minutes
Makes one loaf

1 cup all-purpose
  flour
1 cup whole wheat
  flour
1 teaspoon baking
  soda
1/2 teaspoon each of
  ground cinnamon,
  pumpkin pie spice
  and ground ginger
1/2 cup chopped
  pecans
1/4 cup light brown
  sugar
4 oz butter, melted
2/3 cup honey
1 tablespoon grated
  orange rind
1/2 cup freshly
  squeezed orange
  juice
1 egg, lightly
  beaten

1. Preheat the oven to
warm 315°F. Lightly
grease a 5¹/2 x 8¹/2 x
2³/4 inch loaf pan and
line the base with
waxed paper.
2. Sift the flours,
soda and spices into
a large bowl; return
the husks to the bowl.
Add the pecans and
sugar; mix well.

Orange Poppy Seed Cake (top) with Honey Pecan Spice Loaf

Using a wooden spoon, stir through the butter, honey, rind, juice and egg; mix until thoroughly combined. **3.** Pour the mixture into the pan. Bake for 55 minutes, or until a skewer comes out clean when inserted in the center. Set aside for 3 minutes, then turn onto a wire rack to cool. Ice with a citrus-flavored Buttercream (see page 60), or serve sliced and buttered.

15

Orange and Raisin Ring

Preparation time:
  20 minutes
Total cooking time:
  35 minutes
Makes one ring
cake

1¼ *cups self-rising*
  flour
1 *cup whole wheat*
  self-rising flour
¼ *teaspoon*
  baking soda
1 *cup light brown*
  sugar
1 *cup raisins,*
  chopped
1 *tablespoon grated*
  orange rind
⅓ *cup freshly*
  squeezed orange
  juice
4 *oz butter, melted*
1 *cup plain yogurt*
2 *eggs, lightly beaten*
confectioners' sugar,
  for dusting

1. Preheat the oven
to moderate 350°F.
Brush a deep, 8 inch
bundt or ring pan with
melted butter or oil.
Sift the flours and soda
into a large bowl and
then return the husks
to the bowl.
2. Add the sugar,
raisins and orange

rind; mix well. Using
a wooden spoon, stir
in the orange juice,
butter, yogurt and
eggs until thoroughly
combined.
3. Spoon the mixture
into the prepared
pan and smooth the
top with a spatula.
Bake for 35 minutes,
or until a skewer
comes out clean when
inserted in the center
of the cake. Set aside
for 3 minutes before
turning onto a wire
rack to cool. Serve
dusted with
confectioners' sugar.

Pecan Butterscotch Cake

Preparation time:
  20 minutes
Total cooking time:
  1 hour
Makes one round
cake

9⅔ *oz butter*
1⅓ *cups light brown*
  sugar
1½ *cups pecan halves*
2 *eggs*
1 *tablespoon golden*
  syrup or dark corn
  syrup
1½ *cups self-rising*
  flour
½ *cup milk*

Orange and Raisin Ring (top) with
Pecan Butterscotch Cake

1. Preheat the oven
to moderate 350°F.
Grease a deep, 8 inch
round cake pan and
line the base and side
with waxed paper.
2. Soften 1½ oz of
the butter. Place in
a small bowl with
⅓ cup of the sugar;
mix until smooth and
creamy. Spread over
the base of the pan.
Arrange the pecan
halves, flat sides up,
decoratively over
this mixture.
3. Combine the
remaining butter and
sugar with the eggs,
syrup, sifted flour
and milk in a bowl.
Beat with electric
beaters on low speed
until the ingredients
are thoroughly mixed.
Increase the speed
to medium and beat
until the mixture is
smooth and has
changed color.
4. Spoon the mixture
into the prepared
pan and smooth the
top with a spatula.
Bake for 1 hour, or
until a skewer comes
out clean when
inserted in the center
of the cake. Set aside
for 5 minutes before
turning onto a serving
plate or wire rack
to cool. Pecan
Butterscotch Cake
can be served either
warm or cold.

Italian Cookie Refrigerator Cake

Preparation time:
  15 minutes + 5 hours
  refrigeration
Total cooking time:
  3 minutes
*Makes one round
cake*

6¹/2 oz dark chocolate,
  chopped
6¹/2 oz butter
2 eggs
³/4 cup dried fruit
  (peaches, apricots,
  dates and prunes,
  pitted and roughly
  chopped)
¹/4 cup hazelnuts,
  roughly chopped
4 oz plain sweet
  cookies, broken into
  smallish pieces

1. Lightly grease
a deep, 8 inch
springform pan.
Line the base and side
with waxed paper.
2. Combine the
chocolate and butter
in a small heatproof
bowl. Place over a
pan of simmering
water; stir until melted.
3. Cool slightly, then
whisk in the eggs. Fold
in the dried fruit,
hazelnuts and cookie
pieces, mixing well.
Pour the mixture into
the pan and smooth.
Refrigerate for

5 hours, or until set.
4. Serve cut into small
wedges, with ice cream
or thick cream.

Note: You may also
use an 8 inch round,
loose-bottomed fluted
quiche pan for this
recipe. Make sure to
grease the pan well.

Tutti-Frutti Cake

Preparation time:
  20 minutes
Total cooking time:
  45 minutes
*Makes one round
cake*

4 oz butter
¹/2 cup sugar
2 teaspoons finely
  grated orange rind
2 eggs
1 tablespoon freshly
  squeezed orange
  juice
³/4 cup self-rising
  flour
1 cup fresh white
  bread crumbs
¹/3 cup pitted prunes,
  chopped
¹/3 cup chopped glacé
  pineapple
¹/2 cup dried (or glacé)
  apricots, chopped
1 tablespoon chopped
  mixed candied citrus
  peel

1. Preheat the oven
to moderate 350°F.
Brush a deep, 8 inch
round cake pan with
melted butter or oil.
Line the base and side
with waxed paper.
2. Place the butter,
sugar and rind in a
small bowl and beat,
using electric beaters,
until light and creamy.
Add the eggs one
at a time, beating
thoroughly after
each addition.
3. Transfer the mixture
to a large mixing bowl.
Using a metal spoon,
fold in the orange juice
and sifted flour. Add
the bread crumbs,
prunes, pineapple,
apricots and peel; stir
until just combined
and the mixture is
just smooth.
4. Spoon the mixture
into the prepared pan
and smooth the surface
with a spatula. Bake
for 45 minutes, or
until a skewer comes
out clean when inserted
in the center of the
cake. Set aside for
10 minutes, then turn
onto a wire rack to
cool. Ice with a
citrus-flavored
Buttercream (page 60)
or Citrus Cream Cheese
Icing (page 62), and
sprinkle with nutmeg.

---

*Tutti-Frutti Cake (top) with
Italian Cookie Refrigerator Cake*

Blueberry Cake

Preparation time:
  30 minutes
Total cooking time:
  55 minutes
*Makes one round
cake*

1/2 cup sugar, plus
  1 tablespoon, extra
8 oz fresh blueberries
2 eggs
1 teaspoon vanilla
  extract
4 oz butter, melted
1 1/3 cups self-rising
  flour
2 tablespoons light
  brown sugar

1. Preheat the oven
to moderate 350°F.
Brush a deep, 8 inch
round cake pan with
melted butter or oil.
Line the base and side
with waxed paper.
2. Place 1 tablespoon
of the sugar and half
the berries in a pan
over low heat. Stir
until the juices run.
Stir in the remaining
berries; cool.
3. Beat the eggs in a
large bowl until thick.
Use a metal spoon to
fold in the vanilla,
butter, flour and
remaining sugar,
until just smooth.

4. Stir 3/4 cup cake
mixture into the
berries. Spoon the
berry mixture and
remaining cake
mixture into the pan.
Swirl with a skewer
to marble and
sprinkle brown sugar
on top. Bake for
45–50 minutes, until
a skewer comes out
clean when inserted
in the center. Set aside
for 5 minutes, then
turn onto a wire rack
to cool. Dust with
confectioners' sugar,
if you like.

Custard and Cream Sponge

Preparation time:
  35 minutes +
  overnight refrigeration
Total cooking time:
  Nil
Serves 6–8

4 oz cream cheese
1/2 cup ready-made
  custard
1 2/3 cups cream
1/2 cup strong black
  coffee
1/3 cup brandy
2 teaspoons sugar
8 oz savoiardi cookies

1. Use plastic wrap to
line a 7 1/2 x 4 x 3 inch

loaf pan or dish,
allowing it to hang
over the edges. Beat
the cream cheese until
smooth and creamy.
Gradually beat in
the custard.
2. Beat 2/3 cup of the
cream until soft peaks
form. (Refrigerate
remaining cream.)
Fold into the custard
mixture and set aside.
Place the coffee, brandy
and sugar in a bowl.
Mix well to dissolve
the sugar. Cut the
cookies to fit the
width of the pan.
3. Dip the cookies
one or two at a time
in the coffee mixture.
Place a layer side-by-
side in the base of the
pan. Spread over a
third of the custard
mixture. Dip and
place a second layer
of cookies in the pan.
Top with another
layer of the custard
mixture. Complete with
a final layer of cookies
and the remaining
custard mixture.
4. Fold the plastic
wrap over the top of
the cake; refrigerate
overnight. Beat the
remaining cream until
firm peaks form. Place
the cake on a serving
plate, spread with
whipped cream and dust
with a little drinking
chocolate powder.
Cut into slices to serve.

*Blueberry Cake (top) with
Custard and Cream Sponge*

Frozen Chocolate Mousse Cake

Preparation time:
30 minutes +
overnight freezing
Total cooking time:
30–35 minutes
Makes one round cake

1 cup whole, shelled almonds or pecans
1 lb dark chocolate, chopped
4³/4 oz butter
1 tablespoon instant coffee powder or granules
1 teaspoon vanilla extract
2 tablespoons light brown sugar
4 eggs
¹/4 cup all-purpose flour

1. Preheat the oven to moderate 350°F. Brush a deep, 8³/4 inch round cake pan with melted butter or oil. Line the base and side with waxed paper. Place the almonds or pecans in a food processor bowl. Process in short bursts until the nuts are finely ground. Set aside.
2. Combine the dark chocolate, butter, coffee powder or granules, and vanilla extract in a large pan. Stir over low heat until the mixture is melted and smooth. Remove from the heat. This mixture can also be melted in a large bowl in the microwave. Melt on High (100%) for 1–2 minutes in short bursts, stirring after each minute. Beat the sugar and eggs with electric beaters for 2–3 minutes, until thick and creamy.

3. Fold into the chocolate mixture with the ground almonds or pecans and flour; stir until well combined. Spoon the mixture into the prepared pan. Bake for 30 minutes, or until the top of the cake is set. Remove the cake from the oven and cool.
4. Cover the cake with plastic wrap and freeze overnight. This cake is extremely rich and is delicious spread with Chocolate Sour Cream Icing (see page 63). Or, serve in small wedges dusted with sifted cocoa and confectioners' sugar, topped with a dollop of thick cream or ice cream.

Note: Use a good quality, dark cooking chocolate for this recipe.

Frozen Chocolate Mousse Cake

1 Line the base and side of a deep, round cake pan with non-stick waxed paper.

2 Beat the sugar and eggs with electric beaters until thick and creamy.

3 Gently spoon the mixture into the prepared pan.

4 Bake until the top of the cake is firm to the touch.

23

Pear and Pecan Cake

Preparation time:
  20 minutes
Total cooking time:
  1 hour
Makes one round cake

2 teaspoons lemon
  juice
1 ripe pear, peeled,
  cored and roughly
  chopped
4³/4 oz butter
³/4 cup sugar
3 eggs
1 teaspoon ground
  cinnamon
pinch of nutmeg
1¹/4 cups self-rising
  flour
³/4 cup pecans,
  roughly chopped
¹/4 cup light brown
  sugar

1. Sprinkle lemon juice over the pear. Preheat the oven to moderate 350°F. Brush a deep, 8 inch springform cake pan with melted butter or oil and line the base and side with waxed paper.
2. Beat the butter and sugar until light and creamy. Beat in the eggs, one at a time, then add the cinnamon and nutmeg. Fold in the flour, two-thirds of the pecans and the pear; stir to combine.
3. Spoon the mixture into the prepared pan and sprinkle with the combined remaining pecans and brown sugar. Bake for 1 hour, or until a skewer inserted in the center of the cake comes out clean. Cover with foil after 45 minutes if the top starts to brown too much. Set the cake aside for 5 minutes before turning onto a wire rack to cool.

Brandied Orange and Golden Raisin Cake

Preparation time:
  20 minutes
Total cooking time:
  45 minutes
Makes two oblong cakes

4 oz butter, melted
3 cups golden raisins
¹/2 cup light brown
  sugar
2 tablespoons orange
  marmalade
1 tablespoon grated
  orange rind
2 eggs
¹/4 cup brandy, plus
  1¹/2 tablespoons, extra
³/4 cup all-purpose
  flour
¹/4 cup self-rising flour
roughly chopped
  almonds and glacé
  cherries, to decorate

1. Preheat the oven to slow 300°F. Grease two deep, 3 x 10¹/2 inch loaf pans and line the bases and sides with waxed paper.
2. Combine the butter, golden raisins, brown sugar, marmalade, orange rind, eggs and ¹/4 cup brandy with the flours in a large bowl. Stir with a wooden spoon until thoroughly combined.
3. Divide the mixture evenly between the prepared pans and smooth the surface. Decorate with almonds and cherries. Bake for 45 minutes, or until a skewer comes out clean when inserted in the center of the cakes. Sprinkle the cakes with the extra brandy, cover tightly with foil and cool in the pans.

Note: Brandied Orange and Golden Raisin Cake will keep for up to 3 weeks in an airtight container in the refrigerator.

Pear and Pecan Cake (top) with Brandied Orange and Golden Raisin Cake

Devil's Dark Chocolate Cake

Preparation time:
  15 minutes
Total cooking time:
  45 minutes
Makes one ring cake

2¼ cups self-rising
  flour
1 teaspoon baking
  soda
⅔ cup cocoa
  powder
1½ cups sugar
5 oz butter, softened
1 cup water
3 eggs, lightly
  beaten

1. Preheat the oven to moderate 350°F. Brush a 9½ inch fluted ring pan with melted butter. Sift the flour, baking soda and cocoa into a large mixing bowl. Stir in the sugar. Add the butter, water and eggs. Using electric beaters, beat the mixture on low speed until well combined. Increase the speed to medium and beat for a further 3 minutes.
2. Spoon the mixture into the prepared pan and smooth the surface using a spatula. Bake for 45 minutes, or until a skewer comes out clean when inserted in the center of the cake. Set the cake aside for 10 minutes before turning onto a wire rack to cool. Dust with sifted confectioners' sugar, if you like. Alternatively, ice with Rich Chocolate Icing (see page 63) or Chocolate Buttercream (see page 60), or simply drizzle with Chocolate Sauce (see page 59).

Pineapple and Banana Cake

Preparation time:
  30 minutes
Total cooking time:
  1 hour
Makes one round cake

2 ripe bananas,
  mashed
½ cup drained
  crushed pineapple
1¼ cups sugar
1⅔ cups self-rising
  flour
2 teaspoons ground
  cinnamon
⅔ cup oil
¼ cup pineapple
  juice
2 eggs

1. Preheat the oven to moderate 350°F. Brush a deep, 9 inch round cake pan with melted butter or oil. Line the base and side with waxed paper. Place the bananas, crushed pineapple and sugar in a large mixing bowl. Add the sifted flour and cinnamon; stir to combine using a wooden spoon.
2. Whisk the oil, pineapple juice and eggs together and add to the banana mixture. Stir until combined and smooth. Pour the mixture into the prepared pan and smooth the surface with a spatula. Bake for 1 hour, or until a skewer comes out clean when inserted in the center of the cake. Set aside for 10 minutes before turning onto a wire rack to cool.
3. When cool, spread with a Cream Cheese Icing (see page 62) and decorate with dried mango slices.

Note: Pineapple and Banana Cake will keep for up to 4 days in an airtight container. Store in a refrigerator if the weather is hot.

---

*Devil's Dark Chocolate Cake (top) with
Pineapple and Banana Cake*

Sour Cream Coffee Cake

Preparation time:
25 minutes
Total cooking time:
30–40 minutes
*Makes one oblong
cake*

4 oz butter
1 cup sugar
3 eggs, lightly
 beaten
1 teaspoon vanilla
 extract
1 tablespoon instant
 coffee powder
3/4 cup all-purpose
 flour
1/2 cup self-rising
 flour
1/3 cup sour cream

1. Preheat the oven to warm 315°F. Brush the base and sides of a shallow 11 x 7 inch oblong pan with melted butter or oil. Line base and sides with waxed paper.
2. Beat the butter and sugar in a small bowl until light and creamy. Add the eggs gradually, beating well after each addition. Dissolve the extract and coffee in 1 tablespoon warm water; beat into the mixture until combined.
3. Transfer the mixture to a large bowl. Using a metal spoon, fold in the sifted flours alternately with the sour cream. Spoon the mixture into the pan and smooth the surface. Bake for 30–40 minutes, or until a skewer comes out clean when inserted in the center. Set aside for 5 minutes, then turn onto a wire rack to cool. When cold, ice with Coffee Glacé (see page 61), and decorate with crystallized violets.

Biscotten Torte (Cookie Cake)

Preparation time:
45 minutes +
 overnight refrigeration
Total cooking time:
Nil
*Makes one oblong
cake*

4 oz butter
1/2 cup sugar
2 eggs, separated
3 1/3 oz ground
 almonds
2 drops almond
 extract
2 tablespoons rum
1/2 cup milk
24 sweet oblong
 cookies
1 1/4 cups cream,
 whipped
1 1/2 cups sliced
 almonds, toasted

1. Beat the butter and sugar in a small bowl until light and creamy. Beat in the egg yolks. Fold in the almonds and almond extract.
2. Place the egg whites in a small, dry mixing bowl. Using electric beaters, beat until firm peaks form. Use a metal spoon to fold the egg white into the almond mixture. Refrigerate for 20–30 minutes, until firm but not hard. Combine the rum and milk in a shallow dish.
3. Dip six cookies into the rum and milk mixture. Place the cookies on a sheet of foil in two long rows to make a rectangle. Spread one-third of the almond mixture onto the cookies. Continue dipping and layering the cookies and filling two more times, ending with a layer of cookies. Wrap the cake securely in foil and refrigerate overnight. Before serving, transfer to a serving platter. Spread with whipped cream and top with the toasted sliced almonds.

*Sour Cream Coffee Cake (top)
with Biscotten Torte (Cookie Cake)*

Nutmeg and Pecan Cake

Preparation time:
  30 minutes
Total cooking time:
  35–40 minutes
*Makes one round
cake*

2 cups self-rising
  flour
2 teaspoons ground
  nutmeg
4 oz butter, chopped
1¹/2 cups light brown
  sugar
¹/2 teaspoon baking
  soda
1 cup milk
1 egg
³/4 cup chopped
  pecans

1. Preheat the oven
to moderate 350°F.
Brush a deep, 8 inch
round springform
pan with melted butter
or oil. Line the base
and side with waxed
paper. Sift the
self-rising flour and
ground nutmeg into
a large mixing bowl
and add the chopped
butter and brown sugar.
Using your fingertips,
rub the butter into
the flour mixture for
3 minutes, or until the
mixture resembles fine
bread crumbs.
2. Place half of the
mixture into the base
of the prepared pan.
Press down firmly
using the back of a
metal spoon until
the base of the
pan is evenly covered.
This forms the base
of the cake.
3. Add the combined
baking soda, milk, egg
and chopped pecans
to the remaining flour
mixture and stir until
just smooth.
4. Pour the pecan
mixture evenly over
the crumb base of
the prepared pan and
smooth the surface
with a spatula. Bake
for 35–40 minutes, or
until a skewer comes
out clean when inserted
in the center of the
cake. Set the cake aside
for at least 10 minutes
before transferring to
a wire rack to cool.
Dust with sifted
confectioners' sugar
to serve, if you like.

Note: Cake will store
well for 2–3 days in an
airtight container.
Variation: Almonds or
walnuts may be used
instead of pecans,
if you prefer.

Nutmeg and Pecan Cake

*1 Rub the butter into the flour mixture
until it resembles fine bread crumbs.*

*2 Press half the cake mixture into the
base of the prepared pan.*

3 Add the combined soda, milk, egg and pecans to the mixture.

4 Bake until a skewer inserted in the center of the cake comes out clean.

Carrot and Pecan Cake

Preparation time:
  30 minutes
Total cooking time:
  45 minutes
Makes one square cake

3 eggs
1 cup oil
1 cup light brown
  sugar
1 1/2 cups self-rising
  flour
1 teaspoon baking
  soda
pinch of salt
2 teaspoons ground
  cinnamon
3/4 cup chopped
  pecans
8 oz grated carrot

1. Preheat the oven to moderate 350°F. Brush a deep, 9 inch square cake pan with melted butter or oil. Line the base and sides with waxed paper.
2. Combine the eggs, oil and brown sugar in a large bowl. Add the sifted flour, soda, salt and cinnamon, and beat with electric beaters until the mixture is smooth. Add the nuts and carrot; stir well to combine.

3. Pour the mixture into the pan and bake for 45 minutes, or until a skewer comes out clean when inserted in the center of the cake. Set aside for at least 20 minutes before turning onto a wire rack to cool. Spread with a Cream Cheese Icing (see page 62) and sprinkle with chopped pecans, if you like.

Coconut Cake

Preparation time:
  15 minutes
Total cooking time:
  55 minutes
Makes one loaf

6 oz butter, chopped
  and softened
1 cup sugar, plus
  1 tablespoon,
  extra
1 cup shredded
  coconut, plus
  2 tablespoons,
  extra
1/2 cup buttermilk
  or plain yogurt
2 teaspoons vanilla
  extract
3 eggs, lightly
  beaten
1 1/2 cups self-rising
  flour
1/3 cup cornstarch

1. Preheat the oven to moderate 350°F. Brush a 9 x 5 1/4 x 2 3/4 inch loaf pan with melted butter or oil. Line the base and sides with waxed paper.
2. Place the butter, 1 cup of the sugar, 1 cup of the coconut, buttermilk or yogurt, vanilla and eggs in a bowl and beat briefly with electric beaters until combined. Add the sifted flours and beat on low speed to combine. Continue to beat on medium speed for 1 minute more, until the mixture is smooth and creamy. Do not overbeat.
3. Carefully spoon the mixture into the pan and smooth the surface with a spatula. Sprinkle the combined extra coconut and sugar over the top of the mixture. Bake for 50–55 minutes, or until a skewer comes out clean when inserted in the center of the cake. Cover the cake loosely with foil during the last 15 minutes of cooking to prevent the coconut topping from browning too much. Set the cake aside for 5 minutes before turning onto a wire rack to cool.

Carrot and Pecan Cake (top) with Coconut Cake

Jaffa Cake

Preparation time:
  20 minutes
Total cooking time:
  45 minutes
Makes one loaf

6 oz butter, chopped
  and softened
1 cup sugar
2 teaspoons grated
  orange rind
1/3 cup orange juice
3 eggs, lightly beaten
1 1/2 cups self-rising
  flour
1/3 cup rice flour
  (or cornstarch)
1 tablespoon cocoa
  powder

1. Preheat the oven
to moderate 350°F.
Brush a 9 x 5 1/4 x
2 3/4 inch loaf pan
with melted butter
or oil. Line the base
with waxed paper.
2. Place the butter,
sugar, rind, juice and
eggs in a bowl and
beat until combined.
Add the sifted flours;
beat on low speed
to combine. Increase
the speed to medium
and beat until the
mixture is smooth
and creamy.
3. Spoon half the
mixture into a small
bowl. Sprinkle with
cocoa, mix well and
spread evenly over

the base and sides
of pan. Spoon the
remaining mixture
into the pan and
smooth the surface.
Bake for 45 minutes,
or until a skewer
comes out clean
when inserted into
the center. Set aside
for 5 minutes before
turning onto a wire
rack to cool. Ice
with Chocolate Glacé
Icing (see page 61),
and decorate with
chocolate coated
nuts, if you like.

Maple Pecan Cake

Preparation time:
  20 minutes
Total cooking time:
  55 minutes
Makes one round cake

8 oz butter, chopped
  and softened
3/4 cup light brown
  sugar, plus
  2 tablespoons, extra
1/3 cup maple syrup,
  plus 1 tablespoon,
  extra
1 cup chopped pecans
2 eggs
1/2 cup milk or
  buttermilk
1 1/2 cups self-rising
  flour
1/2 cup all-purpose
  flour

1. Preheat the oven
to moderate 350°F.
Brush a deep, 9 inch
round cake pan with
melted butter or oil and
line the base and side
with waxed paper.
2. Place 2 oz of the
butter, 2 tablespoons
of the brown sugar and
1 tablespoon of the
maple syrup in a small
bowl. Beat with a
wooden spoon for
1 minute, or until light
and creamy. Spread
evenly over the base of
the pan. Sprinkle with
the chopped pecans.
3. Combine the
remaining butter,
brown sugar and
maple syrup with the
eggs and milk or
buttermilk in a bowl.
Beat for 1 minute or
until well combined.
Add the sifted flours
and beat on low speed
until the mixture is just
combined. Increase the
speed to medium and
beat for 1 minute more,
or until the mixture is
smooth and creamy.
Spoon the mixture into
the pan and smooth the
surface. Bake the cake
for 50–55 minutes, or
until a skewer comes
out clean when inserted
in the center. Set aside
for 10 minutes before
turning onto a wire
rack to cool.

Maple Pecan Cake (top) with Jaffa Cake

Double Chocolate Cake

Preparation time:
20 minutes
Total cooking time:
50 minutes
Makes one round
cake

8 oz butter
6¹/2 oz dark
  chocolate, chopped
1¹/2 cups sugar
¹/4 cup whisky
1 cup hot water
1¹/2 cups self-rising
  flour
¹/2 cup all-purpose
  flour
¹/2 cup dark cocoa
  powder
2 eggs, lightly
  beaten
extra cocoa and
  confectioners'
  sugar, for serving

1. Preheat the oven to slow 300°F. Brush two shallow, 8 inch round sandwich pans with melted butter or oil. Line the bases with waxed paper.
2. Melt the butter in a pan. Add the chocolate, sugar, whisky and hot water and whisk until the mixture is smooth. Cool slightly, then transfer to a large bowl.
3. Add the sifted flours and cocoa. Whisk until the mixture is smooth and free of lumps, then whisk in the eggs. Pour into the pans and bake for 45 minutes, or until firm. Allow the cakes to cool in the pans. Sandwich the cakes together with Rich Chocolate Buttercream (see page 60). Dust with combined sifted cocoa and confectioners' sugar.

Note: Can be stored in an airtight container for up to 1 week.

Zucchini and Hazelnut Cake

Preparation time:
20 minutes
Total cooking time:
30 minutes
Makes one ring
cake

1 oz butter, melted
1 tablespoon turbinado
  sugar
¹/2 cup hazelnuts,
  chopped

1 cup grated zucchini,
  firmly packed
1 cup sugar
¹/2 cup sunflower oil
2 eggs, lightly beaten
2 teaspoons grated
  lemon rind
1¹/4 cups self-rising
  flour
¹/2 cup fine semolina

1. Preheat the oven to moderate 350°F. Brush a 9 inch fluted ring pan with some of the melted butter and drizzle the remainder over the base of the pan. Sprinkle the base with the turbinado sugar and half of the chopped hazelnuts.
2. Squeeze the excess moisture from the grated zucchini. Combine the zucchini, sugar, oil, eggs, lemon rind and remaining hazelnuts in a large mixing bowl and stir with a wooden spoon. Add the sifted flour and semolina and beat until the mixture is smooth.
3. Spoon the mixture into the prepared pan and smooth the top with a spatula. Bake for 30 minutes, or until a skewer comes out clean when inserted in the center of the cake. Set the cake aside for about 5 minutes before turning onto a wire rack to cool.

Double Chocolate Cake (top) with
Zucchini and Hazelnut Cake

Raspberry and Passion Fruit Cake

Preparation time:
 30 minutes
Total cooking time:
 45 minutes
Makes one ring cake

1/4 cup all-purpose
 flour
3/4 cup self-rising
 flour
3/4 cup ground
 almonds
6 oz butter
1 cup sugar
1/2 cup fresh passion
 fruit pulp
2 teaspoons vanilla
 extract
2 eggs
1 cup frozen or fresh
 raspberries

1. Preheat the oven to moderate 350°F. Brush an 8 inch bundt or ring pan with melted butter or oil. Combine the plain and self-rising flours with the ground almonds in a large bowl. Make a well in the center.
2. Place the butter, sugar, pulp and vanilla extract in a pan. Stir over low heat until the butter has melted and the mixture is smooth.
3. Whisk the butter mixture into the dry ingredients. Whisk in the eggs until smooth. Pour the mixture into the pan. Drop the raspberries on top, pushing them just below the surface. Bake for 40 minutes, or until a skewer comes out clean when inserted in the center. Set aside for at least 10 minutes. Turn onto a wire rack to cool. Dust with confectioners' sugar, to serve.

Streusel-topped Cardamom Cake

Preparation time:
 15 minutes
Total cooking time:
 40 minutes
Makes one round cake

6 oz sugar, plus
 1 tablespoon, extra
1 cup sour cream
1 egg
1 teaspoon vanilla
 extract
11/2 cups all-purpose
 flour
1/2 teaspoon baking
 soda
1 teaspoon ground
 cardamom
1/4 cup finely chopped
 walnuts

1. Preheat the oven to moderate 350°F. Brush a deep, 8 inch round cake pan with melted butter or oil. Line the base and side with waxed paper.
2. Place 6 oz sugar, sour cream, egg and vanilla extract in a small bowl and beat for 2 minutes. Sift the flour, soda and 1/2 teaspoon cardamom together and spoon on top of the egg mixture. With the beaters on low speed, beat until just combined. Increase the speed to medium and beat for 1 minute more.
3. Spoon the mixture into the prepared pan and smooth the surface with a spatula. Combine the walnuts, remaining sugar and remaining cardamom in a small bowl. Sprinkle evenly over the top of the cake mixture. Use a flat-bladed knife to gently swirl the walnut mixture through a little of the surface batter. Bake for 40 minutes, or until a skewer comes out clean when inserted in the center. Set aside for 5 minutes before turning onto a wire rack to cool.

*Raspberry and Passion Fruit Cake (top) with
Streusel-topped Cardamom Cake*

1 Line a loaf pan loosely with plastic wrap, letting it hang over the edges.

2 Dip the cookies 2–3 at a time in the combined liqueur.

Chocolate Liqueur Cookie Cake

Preparation time:
  30 minutes + 8 hours
  refrigeration
Total cooking time:
  Nil
Serves 6–8

1/4 cup Kahlua, or
  coffee liqueur
1/4 cup Bailey's Irish
  Cream
2 1/4 cups heavy
  cream
6 1/2 oz dark chocolate
  cookies
cocoa powder, for
  dusting

1. Lay two sheets of plastic wrap loosely inside a 10 1/2 x 3 x 2 inch loaf pan. Let the plastic hang over both sides of the pan. The pan is used as a support while assembling the cake.

2. Combine the Kahlua and Bailey's Irish Cream in a shallow bowl. Set aside. Whip 1 1/4 cups of the cream to almost firm peaks. Dip the cookies 2–3 at a time in the combined liqueur. If the cookies are dry and dense in texture, they may need to be left for about 1 minute to soak.

3. Stand a soaked cookie upright at one end of the pan. Spread a little cream onto the cookie and follow with another soaked cookie. Sandwich together the remaining whipped cream and soaked cookies alternately in the pan.

4. Wrap the plastic firmly around the cream and cookies and refrigerate for 8 hours. Gently turn the wrapped cake over occasionally and return to the pan. This ensures that the liqueur does not make one side soggy. Unwrap the cake and place on a serving plate or board. Whip the remaining cream until firm peaks form. Spread the cream over the cake and dust with a little sifted cocoa. Use a sharp knife to cut the cake into diagonal slices. This creates a vertically striped cake.

Note: Chocolate Liqueur Cookie Cake can be assembled up to 3 days in advance. Keep firmly wrapped in the refrigerator and spread with cream just prior to serving. This cake is delicious served as a dessert with fresh fruit.

Chocolate Liqueur Cookie Cake

3 Alternately layer the upright soaked cookies and whipped cream in the pan.

4 Lightly whip the remaining cream until firm peaks form.

Peanut, Raisin and Chocolate Cake

Preparation time:
  15 minutes
Total cooking time:
  30 minutes
Makes one oblong cake

4 oz butter
1/2 cup light brown
  sugar
1/4 cup peanut
  butter
2 tablespoons
  golden syrup or
  dark corn syrup
2 eggs
1²/3 cups self-rising
  flour
2/3 cup milk
3¹/3 oz dark
  chocolate, grated
3¹/3 oz chocolate-
  coated raisins
3¹/3 oz chocolate-
  coated peanuts

1. Preheat the oven to moderate 350°F. Brush an 8 x 12 inch oblong pan with melted butter or oil. Line the base and sides with waxed paper.
2. Beat the butter, brown sugar, peanut butter and syrup in a large bowl until light and creamy. Add the eggs one at a time, beating well after each addition. Beat in the flour alternately with the milk until the mixture is smooth. Stir in the grated chocolate, chocolate-coated raisins and chocolate-coated peanuts using a metal spoon.
3. Spoon the mixture into the pan and smooth the surface. Bake for 30 minutes, or until a skewer comes out clean when inserted in the center. Set aside for about 10 minutes. While the cake is still warm, cut into squares and serve, dusted with confectioners' sugar and with cream or ice cream.

Mandarin and Grape Fruit Cake

Preparation time:
  20 minutes
Total cooking time:
  45 minutes
Makes one ring cake

4 oz butter, chopped
2/3 cup sugar
4³/4 oz chopped whole
  mandarin (see note)
2 eggs
5²/3 oz chopped
  whole grapefruit
  (see note)
3/4 cup coconut
  cream
1/4 cup shredded
  coconut
1/2 cup finely ground
  semolina
1¹/4 cups self-rising
  flour

1. Preheat the oven to moderate 350°F. Brush a deep, 9 inch fluted ring pan with melted butter or oil. Place the chopped butter, sugar, mandarin, eggs and grapefruit into a food processor. Process in short bursts until the mixture is almost smooth.
2. Add the coconut cream, coconut, semolina and flour. Process until smooth. Pour the mixture into the prepared pan. Bake for 35–40 minutes, or until a skewer comes out clean when inserted in the center of the cake.
3. Set aside for about 5 minutes before turning onto a wire rack to cool. Serve the cake warm, dusted with confectioners' sugar. Or, if preferred, drizzle with Citrus Syrup (page 58). Pour the hot syrup over the cooled cake and allow to soak in. Serve with a dollop of thick cream. This

Mandarin and Grapefruit Cake (top) with Peanut, Raisin and Chocolate Cake

cake will keep for up to 4 days in an airtight container. It may also be reheated in a microwave.

Note: When chopping the fruit, remove the peel and cut away most of the pith as it can be very bitter; discard the pith. Chop the peel and flesh, then weigh.
Variation: Use a selection of chopped citrus fruits.

Apple Cake

Preparation time:
  20 minutes
Total cooking time:
  40–50 minutes
*Makes one round
cake*

4 oz butter,
  softened
1/2 cup sugar
2 eggs, lightly
  beaten
2 teaspoons
  vanilla extract
1 cup self-rising
  flour
1/3 cup dried apple
1 large apple,
  peeled, cored and
  grated

1. Preheat the oven
to moderate 350°F.
Brush a deep, 8 inch
round cake pan with
melted butter or oil.
Line the base and side
with waxed paper.
2. Using electric
beaters, beat the butter
and sugar together until
light and creamy. Beat
in the eggs, one at a
time, and add the
vanilla extract. Fold
the sifted flour into
the mixture until
just smooth.
3. Finely chop the
dried apple. Stir the
grated and the dried
apple into the mixture
until well combined.
Spoon the mixture
into the pan and
smooth the surface.
Bake the cake for
40–50 minutes, or
until a skewer comes
out clean when inserted
in the center. Set aside
for at least 5 minutes
before turning onto
a wire rack to cool.
When cold, spread
the cake with Vanilla
Buttercream (see
page 60), if you like.

Molasses
Ginger Cake

Preparation time:
  20 minutes
Total cooking time:
  35 minutes
*Makes one oblong
cake*

4 oz butter
2/3 cup light brown
  sugar
1/4 cup molasses
2 eggs, lightly beaten
1 cup self-rising
  flour
1 cup all-purpose
  flour
1 tablespoon ground
  ginger
1/2 teaspoon baking
  soda
1/2 cup milk

1. Preheat the oven
to moderate 350°F.
Brush a shallow,
7 x 11 inch oblong
cake pan with melted
butter or oil. Line the
base and sides with
waxed paper.
2. Using electric
beaters, beat the
butter and sugar in a
small bowl until light
and creamy. Add the
molasses and beat
until well combined.
Add the eggs gradually,
beating thoroughly
after each addition.
3. Transfer the mixture
to a large mixing bowl.
Using a metal spoon,
gently fold in the
combined sifted dry
ingredients alternately
with the milk. Stir
until just combined
and the mixture is
almost smooth. Spoon
the mixture into the
pan and smooth the
surface with a spatula.
4. Bake the cake for
30–35 minutes, or
until a skewer comes
out clean when
inserted in the center.
Set aside for at least
10 minutes before
turning onto a wire
rack to cool. Ice with
Lemon Ginger Glacé
(page 61) and decorate
with chopped glacé
ginger, or simply dust
with confectioners'
sugar. Cut the cake
into squares to serve.

Molasses Ginger Cake (top) with Apple Cake

Carrot Cake

Preparation time:
30 minutes
Total cooking time:
40–45 minutes
*Makes one oblong
cake*

2 eggs, *lightly
 beaten*
1 cup turbinado
 sugar
1 cup grated carrot
3/4 cup vegetable
 oil
1/2 cup chopped
 walnuts
1/4 cup chopped
 raisins
1/4 cup golden
 raisins
1 1/2 cups all-purpose
 flour, sifted
1 teaspoon pumpkin
 pie spice
1 teaspoon ground
 cinnamon
1 teaspoon baking
 soda
1 1/2 teaspoons baking
 powder

1. Preheat the oven
to moderate 350°F.
Brush a shallow
7 x 11 inch oblong
cake pan with melted
butter or oil. Line the
base and sides with
waxed paper.
2. Place the eggs,
turbinado sugar,
carrot, oil and
walnuts in a large

bowl and stir to
combine. Add the
remaining ingredients
and stir until moistened.
3. Pour the mixture
into the prepared
pan and bake for
about 40–45 minutes.
Cool the cake slightly
before turning onto
a wire rack to cool.
Ice the cake with a
Cream Cheese Icing
(see page 62), if
you like, and
sprinkle with a little
ground nutmeg.

Rich Chocolate Brownie Cake

Preparation time:
 20 minutes
Total cooking time:
 50 minutes
*Makes one round
cake*

1 cup sugar
1/4 cup self-rising
 flour, sifted
1/4 cup dark cocoa
 powder, sifted
3/4 cup chopped
 pistachio nuts
4 3/4 oz dark
 chocolate, *chopped*
4 3/4 oz butter, *melted*
2 teaspoons vanilla
 extract
2 eggs, *lightly
 beaten*

1. Preheat the oven to
moderate 350°F. Brush
a deep, 8 inch round
cake pan with melted
butter or oil. Line the
base and side with
waxed paper.
2. Combine the sugar,
sifted flour, cocoa and
nuts in a large bowl.
Add the chocolate and
mix to combine; make
a well in the center.
3. Pour the combined
butter, vanilla and eggs
onto the dry ingredients.
Stir until all ingredients
are moistened and
mixed together well.
4. Pour the mixture
into the pan and
smooth the surface.
Bake for 45–50
minutes or until a
skewer inserted in
the center of the cake
comes out almost clean.
(The skewer may look
a little moist but the
mixture should not be
raw.) Lightly dust with
confectioners' sugar,
to serve.

Note: The secret of
making this irresistible
cake is in the ingredients.
Using a good quality
chocolate and cocoa
will ensure the most
delicious result. Use a
good, bittersweet dark
chocolate and a dark
Dutch cocoa powder.

*Rich Chocolate Brownie Cake (top)
with Carrot Cake*

Cake Mixes Plus

S tore-bought cake mixes are handy and quick but, above all, can be made into almost any cake you like by adding a few different flavors.

Strawberries and Cream Cake

Preparation time:
 30 minutes
Total cooking time:
 10–15 minutes
Makes one layered cake

1 *Vanilla or Buttercake cake mix*
buttermilk or milk
1/3 cup Grand Marnier or Kirsch
1 1/2 cups cream
8 oz strawberries, sliced

1. Preheat the oven to 350°F. Brush a 12 x 10 x 3/4 inch jelly roll pan with melted butter or oil. Line the base and sides with waxed paper.
2. Make the cake according to the manufacturer's instructions, using buttermilk or milk for the liquid. Spread the mixture evenly into the prepared pan. Bake for about 10–15 minutes, or until a skewer comes out clean when inserted in the center of the cake. Set aside for at least 5 minutes before turning onto a wire rack to cool.
3. When the cake is cold, cut it into three layers and trim each end. Brush each layer generously with the Grand Marnier or Kirsch. Whip the cream until firm peaks form. Spread a third of the cream over one piece of cake. Top with a third of the strawberries. Layer with a second piece of cake, cream and strawberries. Place the last cake layer on top, liqueur-side down. Decorate the cake with the remaining whipped cream and sliced strawberries.

Strawberries and Cream Cake

Warm Chocolate and Marshmallow Cake

Preparation time:
  20 minutes
Total cooking time:
  35–40 minutes
Makes one square cake

1 Chocolate cake mix
3¹/₃ oz marshmallows, halved
3¹/₃ oz dark chocolate, chopped

1. Preheat the oven to moderate 350°F. Brush a deep, 8 inch square cake pan with melted butter or oil. Line the base and sides with waxed paper.
2. Make the cake according to the manufacturer's instructions. Stir in the halved marshmallows and chopped dark chocolate; mix well.
3. Spoon the cake mixture evenly into the prepared pan and smooth the surface. Bake for 35–40 minutes, or until a skewer comes out clean when inserted in the center of the cake. Set aside for

about 10 minutes and then cut into squares. Dust with some combined sifted confectioners' sugar and cocoa. Serve with cream or ice cream.

Note: Use either medium or large marshmallows in this recipe. The smaller ones will simply dissolve into the cooked cake.

Marzipan Cherry Cake

Preparation time:
  30 minutes
Total cooking time:
  35 minutes
Makes one ring cake

1 Buttercake cake mix
buttermilk
¹/₃ cup roughly chopped glacé cherries
3¹/₃ oz marzipan, grated
¹/₄ cup shredded coconut

1. Preheat the oven to moderate 350°F. Brush a 9 inch fluted ring pan with melted butter or oil.
2. Make the cake according to the manufacturer's instructions. Substitute buttermilk for the liquid. Add the cherries, marzipan and coconut; stir until combined.
3. Spoon the cake mixture evenly into the prepared pan. Bake for 35 minutes, or until a skewer comes out clean when inserted in the center of the cake. Set aside for at least 10 minutes before turning onto a wire rack to cool. Serve dusted with confectioners' sugar or drizzled with a Glacé Icing of your choice (see page 61).

Note: The addition of marzipan to this cake makes it moist while giving it a rich, almond flavor.
Serve with a dollop of thick cream.

HINT
Marzipan is available in the shape of logs at most supermarkets. It can usually be found in the cake section or with the sugars.

Warm Chocolate and Marshmallow Cake (top) with Marzipan Cherry Cake

Banana, Apricot and Lime Cake

Preparation time:
25 minutes
Total cooking time:
35 minutes
Makes one ring cake

4³/4 oz diced dried
   apricots
1 Banana cake mix
buttermilk or milk
1 teaspoon vanilla
   extract
1 tablespoon finely
   grated lime rind

1. Preheat the oven
to moderate 350°F.
Brush a 9 inch fluted
ring pan with melted
butter or oil.
2. Place the apricots
in a heatproof bowl.
Cover with boiling
water and allow the
apricots to soak while
preparing the cake.
3. Make the cake
mix according to
the manufacturer's
instructions, using
buttermilk or milk
as the liquid. Beat in
the vanilla extract,
lime rind and then
the drained apricots.
Spoon the mixture
evenly into the
prepared pan and
smooth the surface
with a spatula. Bake
for 35 minutes, or
until a skewer comes
out clean when
inserted in the center
of the cake.

Note: Ice the cake
when cold if you
wish. Use the icing
that comes with the
cake mix and add
3–4 teaspoons lime
juice instead of water
or milk, if you like.
Or, choose a Glacé
Icing from page 61.

Jaffa Muffin Cakes

Preparation time:
   20 minutes
Total cooking time:
   15 minutes
Makes 16

1 Chocolate cake
   mix
2 tablespoons finely
   grated orange rind

Frosting
2 oz butter
¹/2 cup confectioners'
   sugar
1 tablespoon cocoa
   powder
2–3 teaspoons freshly
   squeezed orange
   juice

1. Preheat the oven
to moderate 350°F.

Place 16 paper liners
in cups of one or two
muffin pans. Make the
cake mix according to
the manufacturer's
instructions. Beat in
the grated orange rind.
Spoon the mixture
evenly into the pans,
until the muffin cases
are roughly half-filled.
2. Bake for about
15 minutes, or until
a skewer comes out
clean when inserted
into the center of the
cakes. You may need
to cook the muffin
cakes in two batches.
Set the cakes aside
for about 5 minutes
before transferring to
a wire rack to cool.
3. **To make Frosting:**
Beat the butter and
confectioners' sugar
in a small bowl with
electric beaters until
light and creamy. Add
the cocoa and orange
juice and beat until
well combined. Spread
the Frosting over each
Muffin cake. Top each
cake with pieces of
chocolate-coated,
candied or preserved
orange rind.

Note: The number of
muffin cakes made
may vary according
to the size of the cake
mix used.

*Jaffa Muffin Cakes (top) with
Banana, Apricot and Lime Cake*

Coconut and Caramel Walnut Cake

Preparation time:
  25 minutes
Total cooking time:
  35–40 minutes
Makes one round cake

1/4 *cup light brown sugar*
1/3 *cup coconut flakes*
1/2 *cup chopped walnuts*
1 1/3 *oz butter, melted*
2 *tablespoons golden syrup or dark corn syrup*
1 *Buttercake cake mix*

1. Preheat the oven to moderate 350°F. Brush a deep, 8 inch round cake pan with melted butter or oil. Line the base and side with waxed paper.
2. Combine the sugar, coconut, walnuts, butter and syrup in a small bowl; mix well. Wet your fingers a little and spread the mixture evenly over the base of the prepared pan.
3. Make the cake mix according to the manufacturer's instructions. Spoon on top of the coconut mixture already in the pan. Smooth the surface with a spatula and bake for 35–40 minutes, or until a skewer comes out clean when inserted in the center. Set aside for 5 minutes before turning onto a wire rack to cool. This cake is also delicious served warm with ice cream or cream.

Variation: Use pecans or macadamias in place of the walnuts if you prefer. Shredded coconut can be used instead of coconut flakes.

Orange and Prune Cake

Preparation time:
  30 minutes
Total cooking time:
  35–40 minutes
Makes one square cake

15 *pitted prunes, chopped*
1/3 *cup Marsala*
1 *Orange cake mix*
buttermilk or milk
3 *teaspoons finely grated orange rind*

1. Preheat the oven to moderate 350°F. Brush a deep, 8 inch square cake pan with melted butter or oil. Line the base and sides with waxed paper.
2. Combine the chopped prunes and Marsala in a small pan. Simmer gently until the prunes have absorbed all the liquid. Alternatively, place in a microwave-safe bowl and cook in the microwave on High (100%) in short bursts, for 1–2 minutes, until the liquid is absorbed.
3. Make the cake mix according to the manufacturer's instructions, using buttermilk or milk as the liquid. Beat in the rind and prunes. Spoon the mixture into the pan and smooth the top. Bake for 35–40 minutes, or until a skewer comes out clean when inserted in the center of the cake. Set aside for about 10 minutes, then turn onto a wire rack to cool.

Note: Ice the cake when cold if you wish. Use the icing that comes with the cake mix and add 2 teaspoons of grated orange rind, or choose an icing from pages 58–63.

Orange and Prune Cake (top) with Coconut and Caramel Walnut Cake

Marble Cake

Preparation time:
  20 minutes
Total cooking time:
  35 minutes
Makes one ring cake

1 Buttercake cake mix
1 tablespoon dark
  cocoa powder
2 teaspoons milk
red food coloring
3 teaspoons finely
  grated orange rind

1. Preheat the oven
to moderate 350°F.
Brush a deep, 8 inch
bundt or ring pan
with melted butter
or oil. Make the cake
mix according to
the manufacturer's
instructions; divide
among three bowls.
2. To one bowl, add
the cocoa powder and
milk. Mix gently until
the mixture is smooth.
To another bowl, add
several drops of red
food coloring and
mix well. To the
remaining bowl,
add the grated
orange rind and mix
well to combine.
3. Spoon the three
mixtures randomly
into the pan. Swirl a
skewer through to
create a marbling
effect. Lightly smooth
the surface. Bake for

35 minutes, or until a
skewer comes out clean
when inserted in the
center of the cake. Set
aside for at least 10
minutes before turning
onto a wire rack to
cool. Serve dusted with
confectioners' sugar, or
drizzled with a Glacé
Icing of your choice (see
page 61) and sprinkled
with a little cinnamon.

Chocolate Almond Muffin Cake

Preparation time:
  20 minutes
Total cooking time:
  25–30 minutes
Makes one oblong
cake

1 packet Chocolate
  Chip Muffin Mix
1/3 cup ground
  almonds
1/4 cup sliced almonds
1/2 cup chocolate
  chips (you may use
  either white, dark
  or milk bits, or try
  using a combination
  of all three)

1. Preheat the oven
to moderate 350°F.
Brush a 7 x 11 inch
oblong cake pan with
melted butter or oil.
Line the base and sides
with waxed paper.
Make up the muffin
mix according to the
manufacturer's
instructions. Stir in
the ground almonds.
2. Spoon the cake
mixture into the pan
and lightly smooth the
surface with a spatula.
Combine the flaked
almonds and chocolate
chips and scatter them
over the cake. Bake for
25–30 minutes, or
until a skewer comes
out clean when
inserted in the center
of the cake.
3. Set aside for at
least 10 minutes
before turning onto
a wire rack to cool.
Serve cut into squares
or oblongs. Dust with
a little confectioners'
sugar if you wish.

HINT
There is a wide
variety of muffin
mixes available at
most supermarkets.
For a completely
different flavor, try
using a banana or
blueberry mix.

Chocolate Almond Muffin Cake (top)
with Marble Cake

Icings, Sauces and Glazes

The cakes in this book are delicious enough to eat without an icing or decorations. However, there are occasions that call for something special, so we have included a variety of icings, sauces and glazes. We've pictured some of our favorite decorations to give you inspiration.

Decorating can be as simple as a quick dust of confectioners' sugar or cocoa. Try sifting confectioners' sugar or cocoa over a lacy paper doily, strips of waxed paper or a patterned cardboard stencil. Or you may prefer to finish your cake with a brushing of warm melted jam and brandy.

Try topping your cake with fresh fruits, such as berries or slices of mango. Candies, chocolates, nuts, citrus rinds and glacé fruits also make quick and effective decorations. Just remember the old rule—keep it simple. You'll soon discover that often the cakes that are the least fussed over can look the best.

A drizzle of chocolate or caramel sauce and a spoonful of whipped cream can take almost any cake from teatime to dessert. Serve your cake warm with a dollop of custard or cream and a scoop of ice-cream for a truly decadent after-dinner treat.

Citrus Syrup

1^1/2 cups sugar
1/3 cup lemon,
  lime, orange or
  mandarin juice
1/3 cup water
3 strips of rind
  (use any citrus
  fruit)

1. Combine all the ingredients in a pan. Stir over low heat, without boiling, until the sugar is dissolved. Bring to the boil, reduce the heat and simmer for about 12–15 minutes, or until slightly thickened.
2. Remove the rind and pour the hot syrup over a cold cake, or cold syrup over a hot cake.

Fruit Glazes

Fruit glazes make a delicious, glossy finishing touch. Warm the jam of your choice in a pan with a little brandy. Simply strain the mixture if you wish, then brush generously over the cake.

Apricot and Brandy Glaze

3 tablespoons apricot
  jam
2 teaspoons brandy

Combine the jam and brandy in a small pan. Stir over low heat until the jam has melted. Remove from the heat and brush the warm mixture over the cake.

Jam Glaze

1/4 cup jam
3 teaspoons brandy

Combine the jam and brandy in a small pan. Stir over low heat for 3 minutes, or until the jam has melted and the mixture boils. Strain the glaze, if you wish, into a small bowl. Brush the warm jam mixture over the top of the warm cake.

Clockwise, from top left:
Chocolate Sauce; Caramel
Sauce; Citrus Syrup;
Apricot and Brandy
Glaze; Jam Glaze; Creamy
Chocolate Icing with
chocolate mints

Creamy Chocolate Icing

4³/4 oz milk or
dark chocolate,
chopped
1 cup sour cream

Melt the chocolate
in a heatproof bowl
over a small pan of
simmering water
until smooth. Cool
to room temperature.
Place the sour cream
in a bowl. Whisk in
the cooled, melted
chocolate until smooth
and creamy. Spread
icing over cake.

Caramel Sauce

2 oz butter
2 tablespoons light
brown sugar
2 tablespoons golden
syrup
¹/3 cup condensed
milk
²/3 cup cream

Combine all the
ingredients in a pan.
Stir over low heat
until the sugar has
dissolved, the butter
has melted and the
sauce is smooth.
Serve hot or at room
temperature poured
over wedges of cake.

Chocolate Sauce

3¹/3 oz dark chocolate,
chopped
¹/3 cup cream

Combine the chocolate
and cream in a small
pan. Stir over low heat
until the chocolate has
melted and the mixture
is smooth. Remove
from the heat and cool
slightly; pour over cake.

59

Basic Buttercream Method

Using electric beaters, beat the butter and confectioners' sugar until light and creamy. Add the remaining ingredients; beat for 2 minutes, until smooth and fluffy.

Rich Chocolate Buttercream

2 oz butter
1/3 cup confectioners' sugar, sifted
2 oz dark chocolate, melted

Citrus Buttercream

2 oz butter
1/3 cup confectioners' sugar, sifted
2–3 teaspoons finely grated lemon rind (or lime, orange or mandarin, if you prefer)

Honey Buttercream

2 oz butter
1/3 cup confectioners' sugar, sifted
2–3 teaspoons honey

Chocolate Buttercream

2 oz butter
1/2 cup confectioners' sugar, sifted
2 tablespoons cocoa powder
2 teaspoons milk

Vanilla Buttercream

2 oz butter
1/3 cup confectioners' sugar, sifted
2 teaspoons vanilla extract

Clockwise from top left: Honey Buttercream with chopped Vienna almonds; Chocolate Buttercream with chocolate disks; Vanilla Buttercream with fresh berries; Citrus Buttercream with candied citrus rind

Basic Glacé Icing Method

Combine the confectioners' sugar, flavoring, butter and sufficient liquid in a small heatproof bowl to form a firm paste. Place the bowl over a pan of simmering water and stir until the icing is smooth and glossy.

Passion Fruit Glacé

1 cup confectioners' sugar, sifted
1–2 tablespoons fresh passion fruit pulp
1/3 oz butter

Citrus Glacé

1 cup confectioners' sugar, sifted
1–2 teaspoons finely grated lemon rind (or orange, lime or mandarin, if you prefer)
1/3 oz butter
1–2 tablespoons freshly squeezed lemon juice

Lemon Ginger Glacé

1/3 cup confectioners' sugar, sifted
1/2–1 teaspoon ground ginger
2/3 oz butter
2 teaspoons milk
1 teaspoon lemon juice

Chocolate Glacé

1 cup confectioners' sugar, sifted
1 tablespoon cocoa powder
1/3 oz butter
1–2 tablespoons hot milk

Coffee Glacé

1 cup confectioners' sugar, sifted
1–2 teaspoons instant coffee powder
1/3 oz butter
1–2 tablespoons water

Clockwise from top left: Lemon Ginger Glacé with chopped hazelnuts; Coffee Glacé with chocolate coffee beans; Passion Fruit Glacé; Citrus Glacé with chopped buttered brazil nuts

61

Basic Cream Cheese Icing Method

This is a very soft, thick, creamy topping. Have the cream cheese at room temperature to make it easier to work with. Using electric beaters, beat the cream cheese and confectioners' sugar in a small bowl until light and creamy. Add the remaining ingredients. Beat for 2 minutes, or until the mixture is smooth and fluffy.

Passion Fruit Cream Cheese Icing

3¹/3 oz cream cheese
3/4 cup confectioners' sugar, sifted
1–2 tablespoons passion fruit pulp

Honey Cream Cheese Icing

3¹/3 oz cream cheese
3/4 cup confectioners' sugar, sifted
1–2 teaspoons honey, warmed
2 teaspoons milk

Clockwise from top left: Citrus Cream Cheese with sugared lilac flowers; Honey Cream Cheese with white chocolate disks and mango; Passion Fruit Cream Cheese with passion fruit pulp; a plain Cream Cheese Icing with candied fruit slices

Citrus Cream Cheese Icing

3¹/3 oz cream cheese
3/4 cup confectioners' sugar, sifted
1–2 teaspoons finely grated lemon rind (or orange, lime or mandarin, if you prefer)
2 teaspoons milk

Ginger Icing

2 oz butter
1 tablespoon golden
 syrup or dark corn
 syrup
1 tablespoon finely
 chopped glacé ginger
1/3 cup light brown sugar
2 tablespoons milk
1 1/2 cups confectioners'
 sugar, sifted

Combine the butter,
syrup, ginger and
sugar in a pan. Stir over
low heat until melted
and smooth. Using a
wooden spoon, beat in
1 tablespoon of milk and
enough confectioners'
sugar to make a stiff
but spreadable icing.
Use the extra milk to
make the icing the
desired consistency.

*From left to right: Rich
Chocolate Icing with dark
chocolate curls; Ginger
Icing with slices of glacé
ginger; Chocolate Sour
Cream Icing with
silver dragees*

Rich Chocolate Icing

2 oz butter
3 1/3 oz dark chocolate,
 chopped
1 tablespoon cream

Combine the butter,
chocolate and cream
in a small heatproof
bowl. Stand over a pan
of simmering water and
stir until the butter and
chocolate have melted
and the mixture is
smooth. Cool slightly
until the mixture is
spreadable. Spread
icing over cake using
a wide knife.

Chocolate Sour Cream Icing

6 1/2 oz milk chocolate,
 chopped
1/3 cup sour cream

Combine the chocolate
and sour cream in
a small pan. Whisk
over low heat until
the chocolate has
melted and the mixture
is smooth. Remove
from the heat; cool
slightly. Spread over
the cake.

Index